A Beautiful Mystery

Copyright © Heather Thieneman 2020

Paperback ISBN 978-1-5271-0526-3

First published in 2020
by
Christian Focus Publications Ltd,
Geanies House, Fearn, Ross-shire,
IV20 1TW, Scotland, U.K.
www.christianfocus.com

Cover design & Typeset by Pete Barnsley (CreativeHoot.com)
Printed in Malta

HEATHER
THIENEMAN

A Beautiful
Mystery

WHAT'S UP WITH
MODESTY?

CF4•K

THIS BOOK
BELONGS TO:

Write your
name in the
flashlight's
beam

CONTENTS:

Girls:
A Mystery Worth Solving

When I was a child, I loved to read mysteries. I read as many as I could: Nancy Drew, Encyclopedia Brown, the Mandi series, Sherlock Holmes, Nate the Great…. I read and loved them all. I loved seeing how all the pieces fit together. I loved making sense out of things that didn't seem to make any sense. I loved trying to solve the mystery before the book did. Maybe I got it from my mother. She would read Agatha Christie and The African Lady Detective mysteries. Perhaps you like to read mysteries too? This book isn't a mystery like the ones I used to read, there are no hidden staircases, no secret tunnels, no stolen jewelry and no strange noises. But it is a book that's going to try to get you thinking and maybe will help make sense out of things that right now don't make any sense.

Have you ever thought of yourself as a mystery? You are not a scary mystery like the ones Nancy Drew sometimes tried to solve. But you are pretty complicated and hard to figure out-even for yourself, I imagine! It's what makes girls interesting. If you picked up a mystery and it told you on the first page who did it and why, would you be interested in reading the rest of the book? I doubt it. You also are interesting, because you are mysterious.

But what about if you found a really interesting mystery, yet when you got to the end of the book, the hero died and the murderer got away with it? Would you be glad you read that book? I doubt it. We like happy endings. Girls are not just a mystery, they are a beautiful mystery. There is a happy ending. Something that makes people want to get to know us and love us.

Well, where there is a mystery, there really ought to be a detective. That's where you come in. Again. You not only are the mystery, I am hoping you will also be my detective partner in solving the mystery. Being a detective can be hard work because you have to think hard. But there is an excitement that comes when you learn new things and see how all the clues piece together to make something different from what you expected. There is a bit of a surprise in every mystery. So, if you like surprises, stick around! Because it's time to tackle our first case: The Case of the Ordinary Marvel.

Heather Thieneman
_____, P. I.

_____, P. I.   *Write your name here*

P.S.

P. I. stands for Private Investigator - that's just another name for a detective. Detectives have many names. Later in this book, you'll learn a funny nickname for them!

I am thankful you are looking at this book. Here I will tell you a little about "A Beautiful Mystery" with some thoughts on how you might make the most of it.

I wrote this book as an aid to parents in helping their daughters appreciate the principles and purposes of modesty. In many ways it mirrors the book I wrote for adults, "What's Up with the Fig Leaves?" Some may think that much of this book is not about modesty at all. However, I believe that true modesty is rooted in a deep appreciation for the beauty of the body. Immodesty may be the more apparent danger in our society, but feelings of insecurity and disappointment with one's body are the more insidious danger. The problem is not primarily that a poor body image might lead to immodesty, though it often does: the problem is that in and of itself such a view is an affront to the goodness of God in creation. That is why I spend so much time laying and reinforcing the foundation of the beauty of the human body, especially the female body.

This book does not go into the specifics of what to wear in order to be modest, but leaves it to you as their parents to provide these standards. The goal of this book is to lay the foundation, to explain the whys, while leaving it up to parents to teach the what.

Most of the books I found on modesty for girls were for teenagers but I have geared this for younger girls in the belief that it is much more effective to communicate these truths before they are a big issue. An ounce of prevention is worth a pound of cure, as they say. The fact that I am addressing younger girls has guided both my content and style. I want to encourage them to grow in maturity and understanding, but I seek to do so in ways that are appropriate for young girls instead of talking to them as if they were 10-going-on-16. This book talks about male/female relationships but it does so without going into specifics, that is, without assuming any particular knowledge, leaving that again to parents.

Because of the purposeful lack of specifics in this book and because this material can create opportunities for meaningful discussions, I would encourage you to read this book with your daughter. You will be able to fill in the gaps I have intentionally left and talk about your household standards of modesty and how you came up with them. This will help your daughter to see the concrete applications of the principles she is learning. You can elaborate on male/female relationships as you think will be beneficial. If she has questions, you will be right there to talk with her about them. This book is not meant to be a surrogate, but a tool to help you fulfill your God-given roles as mothers and fathers.

It is my prayerful desire that this book will be a blessing to both you and your daughter as you grow in your appreciation of the loveliness and wisdom of modesty…and a means of strengthening the bond between you.

Warmest regards,

Heather

P.S. I imagine there are some girls who are reading this themselves. If your parents have handed this book to you to read on your own, consider asking them to read it with you. They may not even have seen this note. Or you may have been given this book by a friend. I bet if you ask they will be willing to read it with you and I think you will be glad you asked! But even if they don't have time to read it with you, don't hesitate to go to them with questions. If you don't understand something or if you want to know whether this or that is modest, ask your parents or other Godly adults God has placed in your life. God has given them to you to help you with just such things.

Chapter 1:
THE CASE OF THE ORDINARY MARVEL

Marvels are marvelous things. Astonishing, amazing, impossible things, they are. They make people stop what they are doing and stare in open-mouthed wonder. When their mouths begin to work again, they go around telling everyone what they saw.

However, sometimes people see marvels so much that they seem ordinary or even boring. Mary Poppins was like this. You may have read stories or seen movies about this make-believe nanny who looked after the children of a family named Banks. What were marvels to others, were normal things to Mary Poppins. The Banks children thought it a marvel when they saw her slide *UP* the banister, but Mary Poppins thought it a completely ordinary way to go upstairs. They thought it a

marvel when her umbrella handle started talking, but Mary Poppins simply talked back to it as if all umbrella handles could carry on conversations. When they were left staring with open-mouthed wonder, she would just scold, "Close your mouth. You are not a codfish."

Mary Poppins' life was one never-ending marvel and so, for her, it was completely ordinary and not anything to marvel at. "Do what?" she would ask, puzzled, when someone asked how she did something amazing that no one had ever seen before.

Did you know that you also are a never-ending marvel? Listen to what Psalm 139 says about you and the way you were made:

> For You [God] formed my inward parts;
>
> You covered [knit together] me in my mother's womb.
>
> I will praise You, for I am fearfully and wonderfully made;
>
> **Marvelous** are Your works,
>
> And that my soul knows very well.
>
> My frame [body] was not hidden from You,
>
> When I was made in secret,
>
> And skillfully wrought in the lowest parts of the earth.

One day, in a very secret place, deep in your mother's womb—some place so deep, so secret, that no one could see and no one could help— you were being made by God alone. At first no one even knew you were there! Not your parents, not the doctors! But God knew. And God was making you, forming you, kind of like you might make something out of play-doh. He gave you ears, eyes, fingers, toes, teeth, all while no one else could help him out at all. He didn't need help. God is very good at creating things. He did a good job creating you too.

Maybe you are thinking "Teeth! Everyone knows babies aren't born with teeth!" Well, that's where you and most people are wrong. Babies are

You covered [knit together] me in my mother's womb.

born with teeth. You just can't see them because they are up in their gums and haven't come out yet. But they are most certainly there. This is where so many people go wrong. If they can't see something, they think it must not be there. But God does much of his most marvelous work in secret, where no one can see.

God did a marvelous job making you, working in secret, at first not even letting anyone know you were there. You were His secret. His marvelous secret.

Then—one day—on your birthday as a matter of fact—you were born! And how your parents marveled at you! They couldn't stop admiring everything about you: your tiny fingers, your soft hair, your beautiful eyes…everything about you was marvelous and beautiful. Because you were made by God.

But the same day you were born, a thousand other babies were born. Only a few people thought much about it. It was so ordinary. Reporters didn't come to the hospital to take pictures of this marvel. The doctors and nurses didn't go home saying, "You won't believe what happened today! A baby was born!" Our bodies are one of the

TRUE Beauty

Write out a Bible verse here that shows you what true beauty is.

The Hanging Gardens in Babylon

The Lighthouse of Alexandria

The Great Pyramid of Giza

You are far more wonderful than these!

biggest marvels in the world and yet they are created so often that no one marvels.

When was the last time you marveled at how God made you? You see yourself every day in a mirror so it seems ordinary, there doesn't seem to be anything wonderful about it. Oh, but there is. People talk about the 7 Wonders of the World: The Hanging Gardens in Babylon, the Lighthouse of Alexandria, the Great Pyramid of Giza, but you are far more wonderful than them all. The only reason you are not the 8th Wonder of the World is just that there are billions like you. It is a most ordinary marvel.

Perhaps you noticed that Psalm 139 doesn't just say you are wonderfully made, it says you are fearfully and wonderfully made. "Fearfully made" might seem a strange way to describe a baby! But fearfully doesn't mean you are scary to look at. Fear sometimes means reverence or awe. So to be fearfully made is to be made in a way that makes people full of awe when they see it. It's that open-mouthed wonder again, but this time the wonder is not at the thing made but at the power and skill of the One who made it.

Now when we reverence something, we honor it. We should honor God who made our bodies so wonderfully and fearfully. We should also honor our bodies. If someone you respect and admire gives you a very special gift, you take good care of that gift.

Taking good care of our bodies shows that we respect and admire God. We should think and speak well of our bodies. To criticize the way we look or feel bad about the way we look is to dishonor our body and the God who made it for us.

One way you can honor your body is to take care of it. We can do this by eating good food, getting good exercise, and getting good sleep. These things are good both for the health and for the beauty of our bodies. If someone ever tries to get you to do something that is not healthy because they say it will make you beautiful, don't believe them! God cares about the whole of the body He gave you, its beauty and its health, and so should we.

Complaining about our bodies shows that we have forgotten to marvel. Can you imagine Mary Poppin's umbrella handle starting to talk and the Banks children complaining, "A parrot? Why did it have to be a parrot? I like canaries better." Or watching Mary Poppins slide up the banister, but all the children can do is sigh and think how much better an elevator would be? But that's what it is like when people complain about or criticize their hair, their height, their noses.

Remember that you were not just thrown together at the last moment like a forgotten science project for school.

God spent nine months specially crafting you Himself in a most marvelous way. Far more marvelous than talking umbrella handles. Look in a mirror and appreciate His work.

Because it's about time you were a codfish.

Because it's about time you were a codfish.

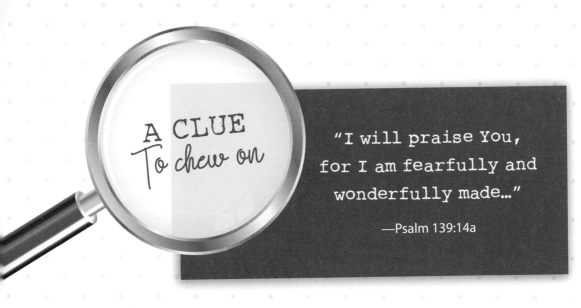

A CLUE
To chew on

"I will praise You,
for I am fearfully and
wonderfully made..."

—Psalm 139:14a

Understanding that we are marvels shouldn't make us proud. After all, we had nothing to do with it! Instead, it should make us praise God.

Take a few minutes now or later to praise God for the way He made you, for your hair, your eyes, your ears, your size, your strength, your beauty.

When you start to feel unhappy with your body, wishing something was different, remember what a marvelous gift your body is from a good and amazing God. Praise Him instead of being ungrateful.

Mysterious ME

From what you have read in the case of the ordinary marvel, why not use this page to write or draw something about yourself

Chapter 2:

THE CASE OF THE SNEAKY LIE

Some lies are pretty easy to spot. If you read a book that says that millions and millions of years ago evolution created the world by chance, I bet you know that that is not true. You won't believe it. You know that God created the world. Parents warn their children all the time about evolution. So you will probably turn the page and squash that lie.

But a good detective is on the lookout for sneaky lies too. Lies that are good at hiding. Lies that are already inside of us. Lies that no one may warn us about. But before we talk about the sneaky lie, let's talk about the truth. The Bible doesn't just say that God created the world. It says that He created a good world. On different days, God created different things, and each time the Bible says the same thing:

And God saw that it was good

*"And God saw that it was **good**." —* Genesis 1

One day He created roses and daisies, apple trees and pine trees.

They were all different, but at the end of the day when He looked at them,

   *"God saw that it was **good**."*

One day He created the sun and the moon, stars and constellations.

They were all different, but at the end of the day when He looked at them,

   *"God saw that it was **good**."*

One day He created goldfish and codfish, canaries and parrots.

They were all different, but at the end of the day when He looked at them,

   *"God saw that it was **good**."*

One day He created lions and giraffes, rabbits and even skunks.

They were all different, but when He looked at them,

   *"God saw that it was **good**."*

He made us in the image of God.

And on one of those days, the 6th day to be exact, God made people. And He made people very special. He made us in the image of God. There are things about us that reflect God in a special way. But this time He didn't just say that it was good, He said that it was VERY good:

> *"Then God saw everything that He had made, and indeed it was very good."* —Genesis 1:31

People are special because we have souls that will live forever. That's one way we were made in God's image. But God didn't give beautiful bodies to roses and canaries and giraffes and give people, His special creation, ugly bodies. He gave us especially beautiful bodies. This is something everyone agrees on. Even people who do not believe in God believe that the human body is one of the most beautiful things in the world. And do you know what else? Men and women both agree that the female body is especially beautiful. We girls, you and I, are the most beautiful things God has created.

Now we are all different. Some of us are short. Some of us are tall. Some of us have light skin. Some of us have dark skin. Some of us have curly hair. Some of us have straight hair. But these are all good things. God did not create anything bad. He did not create anything ugly. Some things might look unusual to us, especially if we are not used to seeing them, but they are still beautiful.

Some people think that some of the things God made are bad or at least not very good. But after creating people and everything else, God said it was VERY GOOD.

God saw everything—not just some things, but everything—and He said that it was all very good—not just good, but VERY good.

It is not enough to believe that God created the world if we believe that He didn't create some things very well, if we think that He did a poor job when it came to creating roses or canaries or giraffes… or you.

You see, the sneaky lie is to believe that your body is not very good. Some people think their bodies are ugly. Some people think their bodies are embarrassing. This is as big a lie as the lie that God did not create the world. Evolution tries to tell us that God did not create the world. Sad thoughts about the way we look try to get us to believe that God did not do a very good job of creating the world. Both are lies. Both are big lies. But one is a sneaky lie that many, many girls believe, without realizing they are believing a lie.

I once had a beautiful cat. She was black except for a white streak going down her front. It reached from her forehead to her tail. It was kind of like the opposite of a skunk. I actually wanted to name her skunk backwards

TRUE
Beauty

Write out a Bible verse here that shows you what true beauty is.

_____

_____

_____

_____

_____

_____

_____

_____

_____

_____

_____

_____

_____

_____

_____

_____

Tux the cat   A Tuxedo

A Skunk

Queen Anne's Lace

Do you think
God would
make a
smelly skunk
beautiful and
not you?

but you can't really say knuks very easily and no one else liked that name, so we ended up calling her Tux because it looked like she was wearing a tuxedo. It's easy to think that a cat is beautiful, but we don't usually think about a skunk being beautiful. We think so much about their smell, that we forget how beautiful God made them. Do you think God would make a smelly skunk beautiful and not you? Would God make the weeds of the field beautiful and not you? It is a ridiculous lie when you stop to think about it.

Now, sadly, the world did not stay good. Sin came and messed things up. Now we do have things like broken bones and scars and, yes, even pimples. These are not good things. These are not beautiful things. But sometimes we will look at our bodies and see them because sin has messed up the good, beautiful things God created. But we should not so focus on what sin has done that we don't appreciate what God has done. There is still much beauty in the world and in our bodies, despite the best efforts of sin. A rose doesn't have to be perfect to be beautiful. A daisy may lose some of its petals and it still gives us much joy to look at.

You are just camping out in the tent. It is not your real home

The Bible says the body we have now is like a tent, but there is a better body coming to those who trust in Jesus:

"For in this tent we groan, longing to put on our heavenly dwelling [house]..."
—2 Corinthians 5:2, ESV

A tent is temporary. It is not meant to last a long time. If you get a hole in your tent while you are out camping, you might be a little upset, but you're not too upset because you know you will not live in it forever. One day you will get home again. Or maybe your tent has a stain and isn't as nice-looking as it once was, but if your real house is a mansion with twenty bedrooms and marble staircases, that doesn't bother you. You are just camping out in the tent. It is not your real home.

The body we have now is like that tent. It was given to us while we are camping out here on earth. But when Christ's followers go to their forever home in heaven, they will get new bodies. And what bodies they will be! They will be more beautiful than the most beautiful actress. They will be able to do more amazing things than the most amazing action hero. It will be like a supermodel and Superwoman all in one!

It will be such a body as would turn even Mary Poppins into a codfish.

It will be such a body as would turn even Mary Poppins into a codfish.

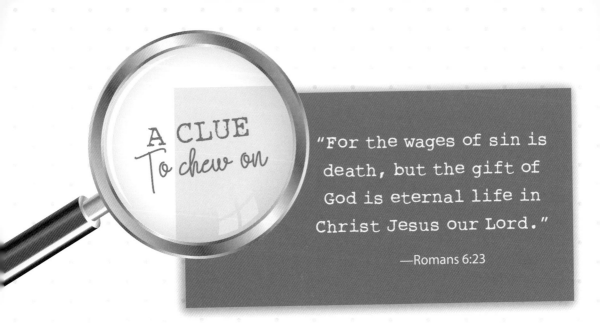

A CLUE
To chew on

"For the wages of sin is death, but the gift of God is eternal life in Christ Jesus our Lord."

—Romans 6:23

Sin brought death into the world. It is because of sin that our bodies, though very good, are not perfect. It is because of sin that our bodies will one day die.

But sin did something far worse than mess up our bodies. It destroyed our souls, our hearts—the part of you that lives inside your tent. Our hearts are not just imperfect, they are very bad. There is no broken bone, scar or pimple that is nearly as ugly, nearly as broken as the hearts we are born with. But God can give us a new heart. There is nothing we can do to earn it, it is a gift. We simply ask for it, trusting in Jesus Christ and his goodness, while confessing we are sinners. With this new heart that loves God most of all and follows him, comes eternal life, where we will get our new bodies and live forever in heaven with Jesus. No wonder they call it good news!

From what you have read in the case of the sneaky lie, why not use this page to write or draw something about yourself

Chapter 3:

THE WHOISIT MYSTERY

You may have heard of a whodunit mystery. That is a mystery where there was a crime and now someone is trying to figure out who did the crime. Whodunit is short for "Who done it?" And I know that isn't very good English but that's what they call it! It can be fun to try to figure out who the culprit is before the book tells you. Well, this chapter is a "whoisit?" mystery. And perhaps you'll be able to figure it out before I tell you.

I'm talking about the whoisit question Snow White's stepmother, the Wicked Queen, asked her mirror:

> "Mirror, mirror on the wall,
>> who is the fairest one of all?"

That's a question many people ask and few people solve. Every year magazine after magazine tries to figure out who is the most beautiful person or who wore the most beautiful clothes to a certain party. But today we're going to solve that mystery, once and for all.

Now, when the wicked queen asked who is the fairest, she wasn't thinking about the man selling tickets to the fairground. She didn't mean the fair that has animals to look at, roller coasters to ride and cotton candy to eat. She didn't mean the "That's not fair!" fair either. The whoisit mystery is: "Who is the most beautiful one of all?"

There is a hymn that uses the word fair to mean beautiful:

> "Fair are the meadows,
>> fairer still the woodlands,
>>> robed in the blooming garb
>>> of spring…
> "Fair is the sunshine,
>> fairer still the moonlight,
>>> and all the twinkling starry host…"

This hymn shows that there are many different things that are beautiful in our world. Seashores are beautiful and mountains are beautiful. Sunrises are beautiful and starry skies are beautiful. Roses are beautiful and daisies are beautiful. But what happens when we try to figure out which one is the most beautiful? Let me tell you a story…

Seashores are beautiful

THE WHOISIT MYSTERY IN THE FLOWER GARDEN

Once upon a time a gardener was walking through his flowerbeds when he noticed something was wrong. The roses looked sad, the daisies looked embarrassed, the tulips' heads were hanging down. The gardener tried to figure out what was wrong. All the weeds were pulled. They were all well-watered. What was wrong with his flowers? It was a mystery to him.

So he went home and got his wife to come to the garden to help him . Perhaps the reason women like flowers so much is because we are a little bit like them. The gardener's wife walked around the garden quietly for a couple of minutes watching the flowers and soon knew exactly what the problem was. The flowers were asking the same question that the Wicked Queen had asked.

You see, Miss Rose was over there pouting by the trellis because when she asked herself, Who is the fairest of them all?, she thought it must be Miss Daisy. Miss Daisy never had a petal out of place, while her own petals were so unruly and seemed to stick out every which way. She felt a positive wreck next to her.

And then there was Miss Daisy sobbing great big tears that splashed on the pebble walkway below. For when she asked herself, Who is the fairest of them all?, She was sure it had to be Miss Rose. Miss Rose was vibrant and her petals were full of bounce, while her own were dull as wash water and straight as a stick. Who would ever pick her when they could have Miss Rose?

Then there was Miss Sunflower who felt like an elephant beside the dainty Miss Grape Hyacinth and just wished she could hide behind one of the white fence pickets. And Miss Grape Hyacinth was upset that everyone thought she was five years younger than she really was while people treated Miss Sunflower more like an adult even though they were the same age.

And, of course, you had Miss Baby's Breath who felt like she had no shape at all and envied Miss Hydrangea and all her curves. While, at the same time, Miss Hydrangea admired the slender, wispy form of Miss Baby's Breath and wished she could cut off half her blossoms so that she could fit in some small bedside vase beside Miss Rose.

Now when the gardener heard what was wrong with his flowers, he was quite upset. He had chosen each flower for its unique beauty. He had put it in the garden exactly where he wanted it and he admired them all. If they had all looked exactly the same, what a boring garden it would be! But as it was, it was a wonderful place to walk around and to enjoy. He liked the straight, sleek petals of Miss Daisy as much as he liked the bouncy petals of Miss Rose. Miss Sunflower, Miss Grape Hyacinth, Miss Baby's Breath, Miss Hydrangea, to say nothing of Miss Tulip, Miss Iris and Miss Lily, all were beautiful to him in their own ways.

The garden that he had created to be a happy place had become a sad and discouraging place. No one could enjoy the beauty of the garden while the flowers were so busy comparing their beauty with each other.

I am very sorry to tell you that no one in that garden lived happily ever after.

Roses

Daisies

Tulips

Sunflower

Grape Hyacinth

Baby's Breath

Hydrangea

Iris

Lily

Have you seen any of these flowes?

Now that may seem like a silly story because flowers would never do that. And, of course, that is true, they wouldn't. But did you know that girls do this very thing all the time? They compare themselves to other girls and start to feel like they're not very pretty because they don't look like this other girl that's really pretty. They look so longingly at the beauty God has given other girls that they forget the beauty He has given them.

Well, you might think that since we all have our own beauty, that our whoisit mystery can't be solved. You might think that, but you'd be wrong. This beauty contest does have a winner. The problem is that we look for the winner in the wrong places. So how should we figure out who is the most beautiful of us all? The wicked stepmother asked the mirror on the wall. And I suppose mirrors would know better than anyone. But instead of asking the mirror on the wall (which in real life can't talk anyway), let's ask the mirror on the shelf.

The mirror on the shelf, you say! What in the world is that? James 1:23-25 says the Bible is like a mirror, it shows us what we are. By reading it, we know ourselves better and see ourselves for who we really are. And if you ask the Bible, who's the fairest of them all, it will tell you. Psalm 45 speaks of a King, a King who one day came to be born in a manger, and it says of this special King:

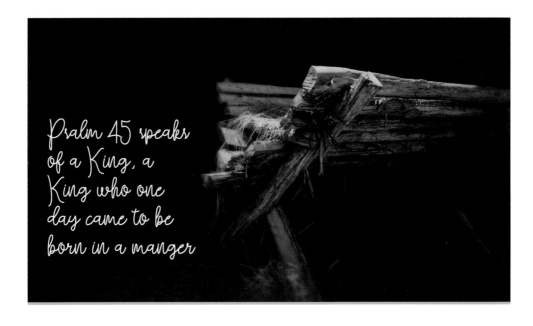

Psalm 45 speaks of a King, a King who one day came to be born in a manger

"You are fairer than the sons of men." —Psalm 45:2a

Have you solved the mystery yet? The fairest of them all isn't you or I, it isn't the Queen and it isn't even Snow White. The fairest of them all is Jesus Christ. That hymn I shared in the beginning is named Fairest Lord Jesus and is about this verse. After describing all the beautiful things in the world, it says that Jesus is more beautiful than all of them:

"All fairest beauty, heavenly and earthly, wondrously, Jesus, is found in Thee…"

The beauty we have is part of being created in His image, it shows a little piece of His beauty. You see, God is so beautiful and wonderful that He had to create many different types of beauty to try to display it all. The rose shows a little bit of His beauty and the daisy shows a different little bit. The sun shows a little bit and the moon shows

TRUE Beauty

Write out a Bible verse here that shows you what true beauty is.

God is so beautiful and wonderful that he had to create many different types of beauty to try to display it all

a little bit. Straight hair shows a little bit and curly hair shows a different little bit. Ever since sin came into the world nothing is perfectly beautiful, but even when our world was perfectly beautiful, there was nothing beautiful enough to show all of God's beauty. So God created many different beautiful things—including you—to show bits and pieces of how amazingly beautiful and wonderful He is.

However, God is so beautiful and wonderful that even all the beautiful and wonderful things in the whole world combined cannot show all his beauty.

Only when we get to heaven will we know how beautiful God really is and it will be truly awesome!

However, I think Satan hates beauty because it reminds him of God. I suppose Satan knows better than we do how beautiful God is. He used to live in heaven with God. He used to be beautiful himself. But not anymore. Now he hates beauty more than the wicked queen hated Snow White and he likes to destroy it.

One way Satan attacks beauty is to make people believe there is only one way to be beautiful and that all the other beautiful things God created aren't really beautiful. Many girls believe his lies and don't like the way they look. They try their best to change the way they look but it is never enough to make them feel really pretty, even though God has made them more beautiful than sunsets or roses.

The truth is that you don't have to look a certain way to be beautiful. Maybe you don't have the beauty of being petite, but you have the beauty of being tall. Maybe you don't have the beauty of curly hair, but you have the beauty of straight hair. The beauty you have is a gift from God, instead of envying the gifts He gave other girls, be thankful for what He gave you.

It was, after all, envy that made the queen wicked. Instead of being thankful for her beauty–and she was a very beautiful woman—the Queen was angry that Snow White had more beauty. Her anger and envy made her try to kill her own husband's daughter. I don't suppose you have ever tried to kill a girl because she was pretty, but you may have disliked or been unfriendly to a girl who was very pretty. Maybe you even wished something bad would happen to her.

So the next time you start to wonder if another girl is prettier than you, STOP.

Don't be like the wicked queen stepmother. Instead remember what the mirror on the shelf says:

"You [Jesus] are fairer than the sons of men."

The next time you start to wonder if another girl is prettier than you, stop.

A CLUE
To chew on

"Anyone who listens to the word but does not do what it says is like someone who looks at his face in a mirror and, after looking at himself, goes away and immediately forgets what he looks like."

—James 1:23-24, NIV

Does it do any good to look in a mirror and then forget what you saw? Maybe a girl looks in the mirror before going to school and sees that her hair is sticking out in all sorts of strange ways because of the way she slept last night, but then she goes right out the door without brushing her hair. What good did the mirror do her?

In this verse, the Bible tells us that it is the same way with us if we listen to what God says but we don't do what He says. Maybe you are your Sunday school teacher's favorite student because you listen so well. Maybe you know all the answers when there are questions at the end. But if you do not obey the things you hear, then you are fooling yourself. Maybe you don't disobey God on purpose, you just forget what He says. You remember it long enough to answer the questions, but then you don't think about it anymore. However, the Bible says that not the forgetful hearers will be blessed, but the obedient doers.

"Do not merely listen to the word, and so deceive yourselves. Do what it says." —James 1:22, NIV

Mysterious ME

From what you have read in the whoisit mystery, why not use this page to write or draw something about yourself

Chapter 4:
THE CASE OF THE RIDICULOUS PIG

Pretend that you are visiting a farm. You see black and white cows in the green grass. You see brown, sleek horses in the stables. You see a few chickens running about pecking at stray pieces of corn. Then you hear loud, grunting noises coming from behind the barn. When you walk back there you find the biggest, dirtiest, mud hole you have ever seen in your life. And in the middle of the mud you see three fat pigs rolling around, snorting and grunting as they roll. They are covered with mud from the tips of their very wide snouts to the ends of their very short tails. You turn to go away before the mud splatters on you when you notice something very strange. One of the muddy pigs has something shiny in its snout. It shines as if it were gold. You look closer. It is gold! A beautiful, expensive gold ring. And then you see, hanging around its filthy neck, a priceless pearl necklace.

That would be ridiculous, wouldn't it? Now let's stop pretending and get to work—detective work. Because there are real cases of this happening. Not just one or two, or ten or twenty, but thousands and thousands of pigs with fine jewelry. And I am sure you have seen them yourself, you just may not have noticed.

How can that be? Get ready for a big word: **Analogy** (*uh-nal-uh-jee*). An analogy is when two things are alike and you learn something about one thing from what you already know about the other thing. This can be a very good way to learn new things. The book of Proverbs has lots of analogies. Do you know what it is like to get a cup of cold water when you are very thirsty? Proverbs 25:25 says that's the same feeling people get when they get good news from friends who live far away. That's an analogy. What you know about cold water helps you understand what you might not know about getting news from friends far away.

Pigs with fine jewelry

The pig wearing jewelry is also an analogy (Proverbs 11:22). You've probably never seen such a pig before, but you can imagine it. The Bible says that is the same thing as a beautiful woman who has poor judgment and makes bad decisions. Her beauty is like a gold ring. But she herself is like a pig! She may be beautiful on the outside, but on the inside she is muddy and stinky. Maybe you have met a girl who looked really nice until you got to know her. After you got to know her, it didn't matter how pretty you had thought she was before. You didn't enjoy being around her anymore than you would enjoy being around a pig wearing jewelry.

This analogy teaches us that what is on the inside is more important than what is on the outside. God says this many different times. He said it to Samuel when Samuel was choosing a new king: "Man looks on the outside, but God looks on the heart." He says it at the very end of Proverbs, "Beauty is passing, but a woman who fears the Lord, she shall be praised."

One way that inside beauty is better than outside beauty is that nothing can take it away: "…your beauty should come from within you—the beauty of a gentle and quiet spirit. This beauty will never disappear, and it is worth very much to God.' I Peter 3:4, ICB.

Have you ever gone to a nursing home and looked at the wedding pictures of the people now living there?

Outside beauty is called passing or vain (empty) because there are a lot of things that can take it away. An accident or a sickness or sometimes just a pimple or a bad haircut. And even if nothing else takes it away, old age will. Have you ever gone to a nursing home and looked at the wedding pictures of the people now living there? It's hard to even tell it is the same person, isn't it? Truly the Bible says that beauty does not last long. But a beautiful heart lasts forever. It can keep growing more and more beautiful no matter what happens.

Inside beauty is also better because it makes people happier. It makes the person herself happier.

Many girls who are beautiful on the outside are not happy on the inside. But a lovely, clean heart brings a special joy to a person. It doesn't mean they are never sad—even Jesus was sad and He had the loveliest and cleanest heart of all. But a beautiful heart will bring you more happiness than a beautiful body.

Inside beauty also makes the people around you happier. It is a little bit nice to look at a pretty face, but it is much nicer to be around someone

TRUE Beauty

Write out a Bible verse here that shows you what true beauty is.

Happy parents

Happy siblings

Happy teachers

Inside beauty
– who will
you bring
happiness to?

with a pretty attitude. Inside beauty will bring happiness to your parents, to your brothers and sisters, to your friends, to your teachers— to everyone you meet. It will also bring happiness to your husband one day. Outside beauty may make a man notice you, but only inside beauty will bring him lasting happiness.

Most of all, though, inside beauty is better because it is what pleases God. He sees our hearts even though no one else can. And He has told us what He wants from our hearts:

> *"'You shall love the Lord your God with all your heart, with all your soul, and with all your mind.' This is the first and great commandment."*
> —Matthew 22:37-38

When you get ready in the morning, what are you thinking more about: inside beauty or outside beauty? Do you spend more time in front of the mirror on the wall or the mirror on the shelf? If you care more about what the mirror on the wall says about you, then you are being like the Wicked Queen. Sometimes we think of wicked people as those people who murder and rob banks. But it is very wicked to care more about what is on the outside than what is on the inside. That's what the Pharisees did and Jesus said some very harsh things to them. He called them white washed tombs. They looked nice on the outside, but inside they were filled with dead bones. Don't be like them! Don't go out with your hair neatly braided but your heart a tangled mess of selfishness, pride and anger. Don't go to church with beautiful jewelry on your ears and wrists, but ugly sins hanging to your heart. Come to God and ask Him to:

"Create in me a clean heart, O God, And renew a steadfast spirit within me." —Psalm 51:10

God made girls to like to be pretty— we like to spend time fixing our hair or picking out clothes, this is good as long as we don't forget that it is most important to have a beautiful heart. Because everyone sees our hair and only God sees our hearts, sometimes we can end up caring more about getting our hair right than our heart right. But if we do that, then we are being a little less like a girl and a little more like a pig!

If you care more about what the mirror on the wall says about you, then you are being like the Wicked Queen

A CLUE
To chew on

"Charm is deceitful and beauty is passing, but a woman who fears the Lord, she shall be praised."

—Proverbs 31:30

King Lemuel had a wise mother and this is one of the things she taught him. It was good advice so he told it to others and God chose to make it part of our Bible. What a different queen she was than the queen in Snow White! This queen mother knew it didn't matter who was prettiest. Beauty wasn't going to last long anyway. And charm may all be a lie. What was to be admired and sought after was a woman who feared God. To fear God means to care more about what God thinks than about what other people think. If you fear God and you know that God thinks that inside beauty is most precious, then you will care more about what He sees than about what other people see.

What kind of girl are you?

Would you be a good wife for King Lemuel?

Do you put thought into how you can please God?

Do you care more about His approval than the approval of your friends or of boys?

If so, then the Bible teaches that you have what is more lasting than beauty and more lovely than charm. You are to be praised!

From what you have read in the case of the ridiculous pig, why not use this page to write or draw something about yourself

Chapter 5

THE CURIOUS CASE OF THE VERY FIRST CLOTHES

Adam & Eve

One thing about detectives is that they can deduce (figure out) things and other people wonder how in the world they could know that. Sherlock Holmes was good at this (Sherlock was not a real person, but a famous detective in books). There are many stories written about all the impossible cases he was able to solve mostly just by thinking. He was always amazing his assistant Watson with the things he was able to figure out about a person just by looking at them.

One story tells about a time when Sherlock came to visit Watson at his home very late one night. As they sat talking in front of the fireplace, Sherlock looked at Watson and said, "I see you have had a busy day at work today."

Watson had had a very busy day, but he was surprised that Sherlock knew that just by

looking at him. How in the world could he tell? So he asked him. Sherlock laughed and told him it was because his boots were clean. Now what did clean boots have to do with anything? But you see, Sherlock knew that Watson usually walked home from work which got his boots dirty from walking through dusty streets. However, if he was especially busy and had to work later than normal, then he took a cab home and his boots stayed clean.

Watson was impressed and cried out "Excellent!" But Sherlock just replied, "Elementary!" He went on to say that it was very easy when you notice details and think about what those details mean.

Now I am not Sherlock Holmes, but I can deduce something about you, something that is true of you this very minute…unless maybe you are the type that likes to read books in the bath, but I very much doubt that you are…

I deduce that: You are wearing clothes right now.

I'm right, aren't I? I can tell by the surprised look on your face that I've deduced correctly. See—they don't call me Detective Heather for nothing. But it's actually quite elementary. Since everyone wears clothes, it is not hard to figure out that you are wearing clothes. But the best detectives aren't content just to know the facts, they want to know what the facts mean, they want to know why something has happened or not happened.

And wearing clothes must mean something important because everyone does it.

Whether you are from America or Europe or Africa, whether you are old or young, whether you are a boy or a girl, whether you are shy or outgoing, everyone wears clothes. I mean, EVERYONE. That's an important clue. The clothes may look different, they may wear a lot or just a very little but everyone wears something. In fact, by the end of this chapter I'm going to help you make a surprising deduction: we're going to figure out what color the first clothes in the whole world were. I wasn't there, no one that I know of has ever said what color they were, but you and I are going to figure it out together, because we're detectives and that's what detectives do. In fact, put on your thinking cap, my dear Watson, and you may just figure it out before I tell you.

Another important clue about clothes is that no one ever forgets to do it.

Everyone wears clothes. I mean, everyone!

Now it is really easy to forget things, even important things like brushing your teeth or combing your hair or putting on shoes. Once I was wearing slippers and I forgot to put on real shoes before going to church! I was halfway there before I realized what I had done. It was too late to turn back so I went to church wearing a nice dress and house slippers!

I was wearing slippers

But I have never forgotten to put on clothes before going outside. I bet you haven't either. I bet you have never had to say on the way to a friend's house, "Dad, we've got to turn around, I forgot to put on a shirt!" Sometimes we may get so busy playing that we forget that we're hungry or that we're tired—or even that we need to go to the bathroom!—but we're never so busy that we forget that we don't have any clothes on. That's how important wearing clothes is.

TRUE Beauty

Write out a Bible verse here that shows you what true beauty is.

Adam & Eve stained-glass window

Figs

Fig leaves

Animals are not embarrassed to go around naked. Only people are.

But here is another interesting clue: animals never wear clothes. I feel pretty sure there has never been a single animal in the history of the world who decided on its own that it needed to wear clothes. If you see a dog wearing a sweater you know that its owner put the sweater on. It's not something that dogs naturally do. If you were out in the jungle and saw a tiger wearing a dress you would wonder which circus it had belonged to and how it had escaped. We know it is very unnatural. It looks strange. Animals are not embarrassed to go around naked. Only people are.

The Bible gives us another important clue: people did not always wear clothes. When God first made Adam and Eve, He didn't make any clothes for them. He made everything that needed to be made in seven days: the sun, moon, plants, animals, people, but no

God had told them not to eat the fruit of one of the trees in the garden but they disobeyed.

clothes. And remember that God looked at it and said that it was good. He didn't come back on the eighth day and say, now it's time to make you two clothes. Nakedness was good. Nakedness was best. Nakedness was perfect.

Adam and Eve spent the first part of their lives walking around Eden completely naked and feeling completely comfortable and unembarrassed about it. They would have thought it was as silly to wear clothes as your pet would. If we put you in a time machine and took you back to the Garden of Eden and they saw you wearing whatever you are wearing now, Adam and Eve would have wondered what circus you had escaped from!

So what happened to change all this? How did something that seemed so strange to Adam and Eve in the beginning suddenly become so important to them and everyone after them? The Bible tells us in Genesis 3. I'll give you a few hints:

It begins with an S.

It has three letters.

It is the ugliest word in the whole world.

Yes, it was because of sin. God had told them not to eat the fruit of one of the trees in the garden but they disobeyed. Before they had been perfect, but now they were sinners. And so things weren't the same anymore. If you have heard of Alice in

Wonderland, it was a little like Alice falling through the rabbit hole: Adam and Eve found themselves in a very different world from the one that they had known. Some things that had made sense in the old world didn't make sense anymore, and some things that made sense in the new world would have been complete nonsense in the old world. Sin changed everything in a way that is hard to imagine, harder even than imagining talking caterpillars and mushroom crumbs that make you smaller and bigger.

The Bible says that as soon as they ate the fruit,

"Then the eyes of both of them were opened, and they knew that they were naked; and they sewed fig leaves together and made themselves coverings."
—Genesis 3:7

Adam and Eve knew they were no longer good and pleasing in God's sight. The main problem was in their hearts, but they did what they could to cover their bodies as if that would hide their sin. They sewed together some fig leaves to make something like a little skirt. Figs are a fruit that grows on trees and the leaves of this tree are some of the biggest leaves there are. Maybe at first Adam and Eve felt better now that they were wearing leaf skirts but when God came, they realized that it was not enough to make them good and pleasing in His sight, so they hid.

God punished them, but He also promised to send Christ to wash the sin away from their hearts.

God punished them, but He also promised to send Christ to wash the sin away from their hearts. God also made them better clothes. Adam and Eve had made their clothes out of fig leaves which didn't hurt anyone, but God made their clothes out of animal skins and that cost an animal its life. Before this, no animal had ever died. It had been a perfect world, where nothing ever died. People, animals, flowers, everything lived forever in Eden. But because of sin changing the world, something had to die to cover the shame of Adam and Eve's nakedness.

Clothes covered it, but they didn't fix it. Many years later Jesus Christ came and died so that everyone who trusts in Him will have the badness of their hearts covered with his goodness.

This is what it means to be clothed in Christ's righteousness. His goodness is like a white robe for our hearts.

Clothes are good but they remind us that something bad happened. It is like a hospital. Hospitals are good, but they also remind us that bad things happen to people. So though it is good to wear clothes, it reminds us of something bad. It reminds us that our hearts are sick and need to be made better. It reminds us that our hearts are naked and need to have clothes on them. Every time we get dressed in the morning, we should remember that we need to be dressed in Christ's righteousness.

Now, Watson, have you figured out what color the first clothes were yet? Think through the clues we know:

Clue #1:

We know Adam and Eve were the first people in the world.

Clue #2:

We know they made their first set of clothes.

Clue #3:

We know they used fig leaves to make their clothes.

Think it through and I bet you can figure it out— because it really is elementary, my dear Watson.

(The answer is written upside down on the bottom of this page.)

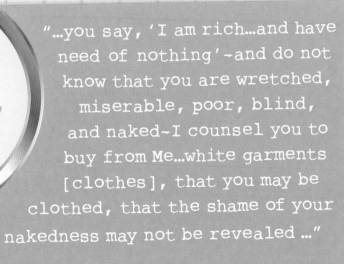

People don't go to a hospital if they think they are healthy. Sometimes people don't want to admit they are sick because they hate doctors. Or they know they are sick, but try to cure themselves because if they go to the hospital, they'll have to give up doing what they want to do, eating what they want and wearing what they want. So they keep struggling on even as they get sicker and sicker. The best hospital in the world may be right next door, but it can't help people if they won't go to it.

Jesus is like that hospital. And the people Jesus was speaking to in Revelation 3 were like those sick people. They didn't think they needed Him. They didn't feel the need for the white robe of Jesus' goodness because they thought they were fully clothed in their own goodness. Or maybe they thought they could use a little extra righteousness, but they didn't realize that they were completely naked. Jesus will give His righteousness to anyone who trusts Him, but most people think they are pretty good on their own so they don't come to Jesus.

Have you ever understood that you are completely naked of true goodness? I mean, as naked as a newborn baby? Maybe you have thought you just needed a pair of socks or a hat of goodness from Jesus but that you had the rest covered. But that's a lie. It is worse than the sneaky lie, it is a deadly lie. It is the lie that has taken more people to hell than any other. You will never come to Jesus for real until you realize that you are naked of anything good. Ask God to show you how naked you are.

From what you have read in the curious case of the very first clothes, why not use this page to write or draw something about yourself

Chapter 6:
THE MYSTERY WITH A HAPPY ENDING

Do you remember the first wedding you went to? After the wedding there was probably a reception. That's where they have the cake. And—Oh!—what a cake it was! I bet it was the most beautiful cake you had ever seen. The only thing was, no one seemed to want to eat any of it! You sure did, maybe you wanted the piece at the top with the little man and woman stuck in the icing, but there was no way to get a piece.

There may also have been a table full of delicious-smelling food. You were so hungry and would have loved some of it. The only thing was, it was all covered up and people in white jackets were standing guard over it!

Maybe you noticed a special table at the front of the room. It had the prettiest flowers of all the tables. Maybe there were bows on the backs of the chairs. The only thing was, no one seemed to want to sit there! Maybe you wanted to, but your parents chose another table that was nice, but not nearly as pretty. You may have been too little to read the elegant white sign with black fancy letters which said simply:

RESERVED

So, to you at the time, it all seemed most mysterious:

A beautiful cake no one wanted to eat.

A beautiful table no one wanted to sit at.

Delicious smelling food no one was allowed to eat.

What kind of party was this?

A lovely Wedding cake!

But then after waiting F O R E V E R, suddenly everyone got quiet and looked toward the door. You looked too. You saw the bride and groom smiling the biggest smiles as they walked in. Then the men in the nice suits and the women in the beautiful long dresses came in smiling almost as big. They all sat down at The Most Beautiful Table. The guards in white jackets brought them The Most Delicious-Smelling Food and they started eating. Then everyone else got some, including you. As you ate, you heard lots of laughing, much of it coming from The Most Beautiful Table. Later the bride and groom came to The Most Beautiful Cake. They cut a small piece together and smiled and laughed. They fed each other bites of it and smiled and laughed some more. Then someone else cut the rest of it and you finally got a piece. I imagine it wasn't the top piece that you wanted, but I hope it was an end piece with lots of frosting. I would also say that I hoped it tasted as good as it looked!

Now the mystery was solved. Everyone was waiting for something very special and very happy.

Not all mysteries have such happy endings, but it is nice when they do. And I have another such mystery to tell you about. Another mystery with a happy ending. I'll give you some hints:

Later the bride and groom came to the most beautiful cake.

It's a three letter word.

It starts with Y.

It is reading this book right now.

It is You.

Yes, you!

You are a mystery with a happy ending. You see, your body is like a mystery. In a mystery, you know some things, but other things you don't know. Your body is the same way. Some parts people can see, but some parts are hidden under your clothes. They are like a mystery. The Bible talks about this mystery:

> *"…on those parts of the body that we think less honorable we bestow the greater honor, and our unpresentable parts are treated with greater modesty …"*
> —1 Corinthians 12:23, ESV

This verse teaches us that some parts of our body are not meant to be seen by everyone. To most people they will always be a mystery. It calls these parts of our body our "unpresentable" parts. Have your parents ever told you to go make yourself presentable? They mean that you need to be ready to have people see you. Maybe your hair needed to be brushed or you were still in your pajamas. When

TRUE *Beauty*

Write out a Bible verse here that shows you what true beauty is.

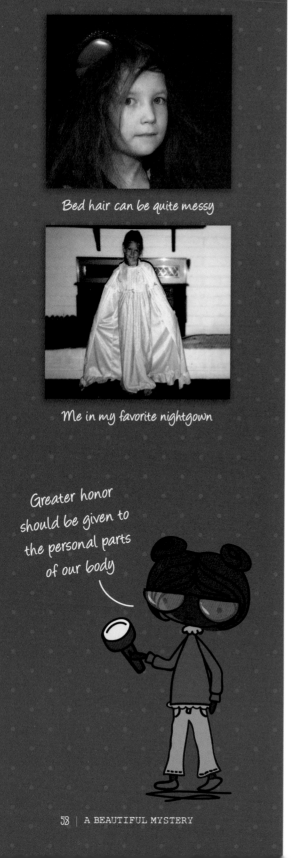

Bed hair can be quite messy

Me in my favorite nightgown

Greater honor should be given to the personal parts of our body

you are presentable, you are ready to be seen. Some parts of our body are unpresentable, so they must be covered up before we are ready to be seen. We often call these our private parts. Just like we don't share our private thoughts with everyone, so we don't show our private parts to everyone. Private things are special and personal. Because these are personal, you can say no if someone wants to see or touch them. It doesn't matter if the person is your good friend, or your parent's best friend or someone in your own family, these are your personal parts and they belong to you.

Now when you brush your hair to make yourself presentable, it is because bed hair can be quite messy, it can stick out in the silliest ways! Our personal parts are not like that, they are not messy or silly, they are more like our pajamas. You may have the cutest pajamas in the world, but you still don't wear them when you go to the grocery store.

My favorite gift as a child was the nightgown I got for my eighth birthday. It was light blue and silky, with a little bit of lace, and reached my toes. I felt like a princess when I wore it and I would go twirling around the house. Yet I didn't leave the house in it. I thought it was the most beautiful thing I owned, but I didn't wear it to go places. It was beautiful, but not presentable. I did, though, have a slumber party that year and was so happy to wear it so that my friends could see it!

Your personal parts are like that nightgown. They are not presentable, because they are not meant to be seen, but they are absolutely beautiful and lovely and can be exciting to show off when the time is right. People cover these parts because they are so very special and are only for certain people to see, especially the husband you may have one day.

I Corinthians 12:23 also says that greater honor should be given to the personal parts of our body. One way we honor them is by not letting just anyone touch them. You see, there are ways of touching that honor these parts. Medical schools try to teach doctors these ways so that they can help people be healthy. But some ways of touching dishonor them. If someone is touching you in a way that doesn't seem to honor your personal parts, you should tell your parents or another adult you trust. To honor something is to treat it with respect, that means, in a way that respects that these are parts of YOUR body that GOD made. If a person is not honoring God and what He wants or if they are not honoring you and what you want, then they are not honoring your body and they should be stopped.

Another way we honor the personal parts of our body and their special beauty is by putting clothes on them. Clothes are like the reserved sign on that table we talked about at the wedding. It wasn't put on that table because it was an old, icky table that no one wanted to sit at. No, it was the most beautiful table in the room and everyone would want to sit at it, but the reserved sign let people know that it was meant for someone else. Clothes do the same thing. They cover the most beautiful parts of you so that not just anyone can look at them.

And that's the happy ending: the personal parts of your body are for a very happy purpose when you are married. Today you may not understand this, just like you used not to understand why no one was sitting at the most beautiful table or eating the most beautiful cake, but one day you will understand. And then you will smile and laugh like you have never smiled and laughed before!

A CLUE To chew on

"For no one ever hated his own flesh, but nourishes and cherishes it, just as the Lord does the church. For we are members of His body, of His flesh and of His bones ... This is a great mystery, but I speak concerning Christ and the church."

—Ephesians 5:29-30, 32

When the Bible says church, it is not speaking of a building but of everyone who loves and trusts in Christ. Do you want to know how much God cares about His people? He cares about them as much as you care about your body. Are you sad when your foot hurts? He is grieved when we hurt. Do you give your body the food and sleep it needs? He gives us what we need.

If you are trusting Christ to save you, you are not just part of His body, the Bible says you are also part of His bride. But right now is like the beginning of the wedding reception. There is much that we are waiting for, much that doesn't make sense. Sometimes it may not seem like such a great party after all. But just wait, because this is the great mystery of all time. Wait until the groom, Jesus, comes back and takes us to the place He has been preparing for us. Wait until everyone has arrived at the party in heaven. Wait until it is time for the Wedding Feast of the Lamb to begin. Then, THEN you will see people smiling and laughing as no one has ever smiled or laughed before!

Because the greatest of all mysteries has the happiest of all endings.

Mysterious ME

From what you have read in the mystery with a happy ending, why not use this page to write or draw something about yourself

Chapter 7:

A CASE OF MISTAKEN IDENTITY

Sometimes words have more than one meaning. If you have ever read an Amelia Bedelia book then you know how much confusion this can cause. I remember reading where Amelia was asked to ice a cake.

What do you think she did? She got ice and put the ice on the cake! Or once she was playing baseball and her teammates shouted "Go for a home run!" Well, Amelia did just that. She went running home—the home where she lived! So sometimes we say words like home and ice but we don't mean the normal home or ice.

To be a good detective you have to pay attention to things like this. It may be funny to read books about people who

misunderstand words, but it is not usually so funny in real life. How would you like it if your birthday cake was soggy because ice was melting all over it instead of having a yummy vanilla icing?

People can have mistaken ideas about modesty too. Some people think it means boring or old -fashioned.

Some people think it is a certain style of clothes. Some people think it is something parents made up to make their children dress the way they want them to! To find the true identity of modesty, it is helpful to know where the word came from. Did you know that words are born? None of the words we use today have been around forever, they were all born at some point in history. Let's investigate how the word was born and how it grew up to become the word it is today.

Hitting a home run

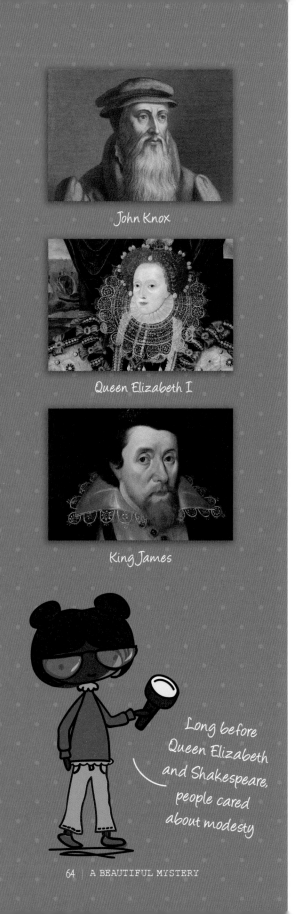

John Knox

Queen Elizabeth I

King James

Long before Queen Elizabeth and Shakespeare, people cared about modesty

If we could take a time machine and go back 500 years, back to when John Knox was preaching sermons and Queen Elizabeth was the ruler of England, we might hear someone say modest for the very first time. But the person would have used it a little differently than we usually use it today. He might have told his son "Don't brag so much, be modest." Back in Queen Elizabeth's day to be modest meant you didn't think you were better than you really were or talk about yourself too much. It was similar to being humble. It still means that today too, but it also has other meanings.

After a while people began using the word modest to describe women who didn't brag about themselves, who didn't show off in front of men to try to get their attention. People thought a modest woman was one who truly cared about men instead of only pretending to care in order to get what they wanted. Parents told their sons to find a modest woman to marry and wise sons listened and were happy that they did.

Then, around the time Shakespeare was writing plays and King James was ruling England people began calling it modest when a woman dressed in

The New Testament was written in Greek so it used strange sounding words like ...

Euschemosune
Kosmios
Aidos

a way that was not trying to get the attention of men. They saw that there was a way to brag with your clothes as well as to brag with your mouth and they thought the modest woman should not do either one.

Today when people talk about modesty they often mean dressing in a way that is not showy, that does not show off parts that should not be shown to everyone. You may hear someone say, "That skirt is too short; it is not modest" or "It is so hard to find a modest bathing suit." They are saying that the clothes are showing off things they shouldn't be showing off.

Of course, long before Queen Elizabeth and Shakespeare, people

cared about modesty, even if they didn't use the word. The Bible talks about modesty several times, but when it was written it did not use the word modesty. The New Testament was written in Greek so it used strange sounding words like kosmios and euschemosune and aidos. Try saying that five times fast! Come to think of it, try saying it even one time slow!

Thankfully the Bible was translated from Greek into English and one of the places they used the word modesty is in 1 Timothy 2 (before that the word was aidos—aren't you glad for translators!):

"I desire then that in every place the men should pray, lifting holy

hands without anger or quarreling; likewise also that women should adorn themselves in respectable apparel [apparel is a fancy word for clothes]*, with modesty and self-control, not with braided hair and gold or pearls or costly attire ..."*
—1 Timothy 2:8-9, ESV

To adorn something is to put something on it, especially something that makes it more beautiful. It is kind of like decorating. Have you ever put some flowers on a table? You were adorning the table. When we put clothes on, we are adorning our body. But what kind of clothes should we adorn our bodies with? Note what the Bible says: respectable clothes, which show modesty and self-control.

The word modesty here means knowing and feeling what is shameful and staying away from it. Shame is the opposite of honor. In the last chapter we saw that we honor our personal parts by putting clothes on them. If we did not do that, it would be dishonorable, it would be shameful. Some people delight in shameful things, but a modest person does not. Other people are ashamed of their bodies, but a modest person is not that either. Modesty means honoring the body. The clothes we wear are an important way of doing that.

Have you ever put some flowers on a table? You were adorning the table.

These verses also teach that we should dress with self-control. Self-control means that we control ourselves instead of doing what we feel like. We may not always want to wear modest clothing. We may want to wear the same things our friends are wearing. Self-control helps us honor our body when it is hard, when it is not what we want to do.

We can either listen to the world about how to adorn our bodies or we can listen to God. Sometimes people think modest clothes are ugly because they have let movies, magazines or their friends tell them what is beautiful. When we believe God's Word, we know that only what honors our bodies really adorns our bodies.

Now hopefully you won't be like Amelia Bedelia when someone talks about modesty but you will know what modesty really means!

TRUE
Beauty

Write out a Bible verse here that shows you what true beauty is.

A CLUE To chew on

"...women should adorn themselves in respectable apparel, with modesty and self-control, not with braided hair and gold or pearls or costly attire, but with ... good works."

—1 Timothy 2:8-10, ESV

The Bible teaches us that true beauty does not come from gold or pearls, or anything we wear, but from doing good to others. People like to say that diamonds are a girl's best friend. They mean that women love diamonds and getting one makes them happy.

But the Bible teaches us that showing kindness by helping others is a better best friend.

You can usually guess who someone's best friend is by how much time they spend together. Do you live in such a way that people would guess that doing good is your best friend? Ask God to help you love good works more than you love expensive jewelry or pretty clothes.

From what you have read in a
case of mistaken identity, why
not use this page to write or draw
something about yourself

Chapter 8:

THE CASE OF JACK SPRAT

You may have heard the nursery rhyme about Jack Sprat and his wife, Joan. It goes like this:

Jack Sprat could eat no fat
His wife could eat no lean
And so betwixt the two of them
They licked the platter clean

Jack ate all the lean,
Joan ate all the fat.
The bone they picked it clean,
Then gave it to the cat

Jack Sprat and his wife make a good case study. A case study is when you study a person or situation and then learn something from that example. A case study isn't trying to figure out who did what, but why things happened the way they did and how they might happen the same way for other people.

Here are the facts of the case study on Jack and Joan:

- Jack and Joan are married.
- Jack ate only lean meat.
- Joan ate only fat.
- Together they ate everything (except the bone, which the cat got!).

Think about a close friend

Are you and your best friend similar?

If someone was exactly like us, we would soon fight, or at least be bored!

The thing we notice from this is that Jack and his wife liked different things and that that made it possible for them to share a plate of food happily. What do you think would have happened if Joan had also liked the lean meat? They might have fought over it, right? Or at least the fat would have been wasted. This case study shows us that they were happy together because they were opposite from each other. Jack liked lean meat and Joan liked the fat. That's why they shared a plate of food happily without fighting and without throwing food away.

This is not just true of Jack and Joan, it is true of other people as well. That's why it makes a good case study.

Sometimes we think that people who are most like each other will get along best, but that's not usually true.

Think about a close friend. She may be like you in some ways, but I bet she is different from you in many other ways. There is a saying that "opposites attract." That means that we like to be around people who are different from us. If someone was exactly like us, we would soon fight. Or at least be bored.

God knew this about people. It's how He made us. So when God wanted to make a life partner for Adam He didn't make another man like Adam. The Bible says:

> Then the LORD God said, "It is not good that the man should be alone; I will make him a helper fit for him."
> —Genesis 2:18, ESV

That helper was Eve. Eve was fitted for Adam. I bet you have made a bed before. And I bet you know that the first thing you have to do is to put the fitted sheet on. A fitted sheet is not like the top sheet. It has to fit the bed exactly to work. It can't be a little too big or too small. It has to be just right.

Eve was just right for Adam. She was equal to him, but different from him.

That word "fit" also means parallel. Eve was a helper "parallel" to Adam. Two lines that are parallel are facing each other. So you could also say that a woman is the mirror image of a man, exactly like him in some ways and exactly opposite of him in other ways. But all with the goal of being fitted to him. This is why men and women like to marry each other. If they were exactly the same, marriage would be really boring.

There is one special way God made men and women different that helps them to be happy together. God made men to enjoy looking at women and

I bet you have made a bed before. And I bet you know that the first thing you have to do is to put the fitted sheet on.

thinking about how pretty they are. You might like to do that too, but men REALLY like it, in a different way than you do. And God made women the opposite, just like Jack Sprat's wife was the opposite of him. God made women to like to be looked at and have people, especially men, think about how pretty they are.

Women especially like to look pretty when they are around men they love. If your mother is just around you all day, she may not put on her best clothes or fix her hair nicely. But I bet she does when she goes out to dinner with just your Dad. And I bet your Dad notices what she looks like and says something admiring! And do you know what else? God also made girls

prettier than boys. I mean, He made us WAY prettier.

In fact, there is a whole book of the Bible that mostly talks about how pretty a woman is!

And it was written by a man! We'll learn more about that book later.

God made men and women to like opposite things and this helps them to be happy together. The husband is happy because he likes to look at a pretty woman and the wife is happy because she likes feeling pretty and being admired by her husband. God is very wise to think of all of this and He is very kind to care about all of this.

Women especially like to look pretty when they are around men they love ...

... I bet your Dad notices what she looks like and says something admiring!

There are so many things that God does for us that we don't even think about or even realize.

The more we learn about things, the more we have reason to thank Him! And that's what all truly good detectives do a lot, they praise God.

Give God thanks for making girls and boys different from each other so that they can grow up and share a special happiness in marriage.

Give God thanks for making girls and boys different from each other so that they can grow up and share a special happiness in marriage.

TRUE
Beauty

Write out a Bible verse here that shows you what true beauty is.

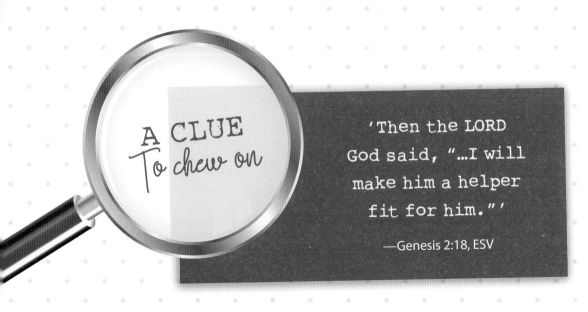

A CLUE
To chew on

'Then the LORD
God said, "...I will
make him a helper
fit for him."'

—Genesis 2:18, ESV

When God made woman for man, He didn't make her to be a ruler fit for him or a trainer fit for him or a teacher fit for him, but a helper. Women sometimes have a hard time with this. They would rather change a man to be what they want him to be. It takes humility and dying to self to be a helper.

But since Jesus came to serve, and since the Holy Spirt came to be our helper, then we should be willing to serve and be helpers too.

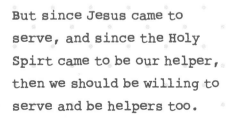

All Christians are called to be servants, whether they are women or not, whether they are married or not. Instead of doing what you want, look for ways to help others with what they need. Instead of pleasing yourself, please God by serving others.

Mysterious ME

From what you have read in the case of Jack Sprat, why not use this page to write or draw something about yourself

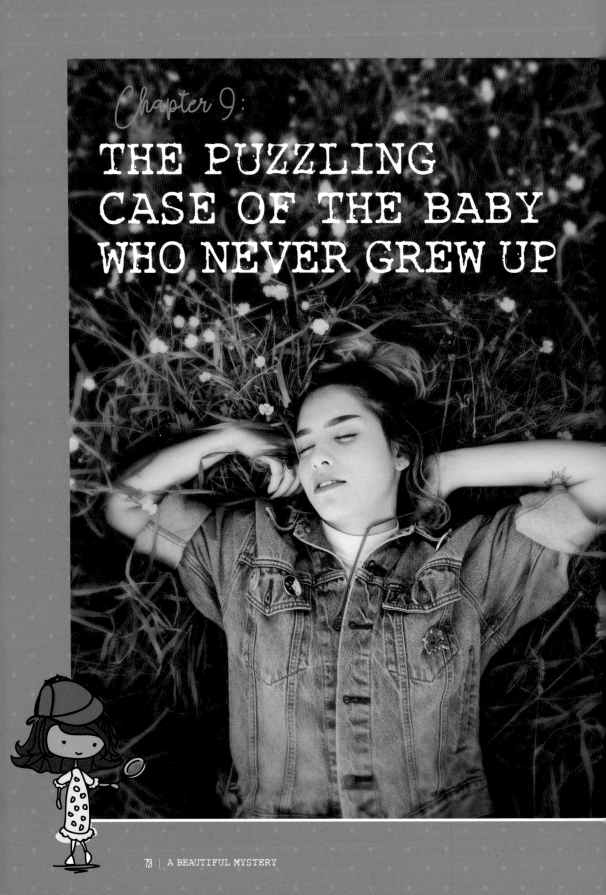

Chapter 9:

THE PUZZLING CASE OF THE BABY WHO NEVER GREW UP

Interesting things happen when we get older. Things we used to like, we don't like anymore. Things we used not to like, we start to love.

I'll tell you a secret: adults like to take naps. That may seem very strange to you, but it's true! Most adults would love to take a nap. Ask them! And when you get older you'll probably want to take naps too.

Here's something else that changes: When you were a baby you wanted to nurse. If you couldn't, my, how you would cry! Ask your mother, if you don't believe me! But now do you cry and cry to nurse? I sure hope not! You changed as you grew up. And it's a good thing!

You are still growing up, your body is still changing. It is changing in ways that will make it more and

more beautiful, especially to men. King Solomon wrote a song about the beauty of a woman he loved and he described her breasts like clusters of fruit in a palm tree (Song of Solomon 7:7). In another book of the Bible, Solomon talked to his son about how much he would enjoy his wife's breasts (Proverbs 5:19). God gives different breasts to different women, just like He gives different hair, different heights and different color eyes, but all are beautiful. Your breasts will be beautiful too.

Maybe you think that you don't want to grow up, you don't want to change.

Adults like to take naps

Mother feeding a baby

Ice cream sundae

Aren't you glad you don't drink milk all day long anymore? Now you get to eat pizza and ice cream?

I bet you felt the same way when you were a baby. Babies don't want to change; they just want to nurse forever and ever. But aren't you glad you don't drink milk all day long anymore? That now you get to eat pizza and ice cream? Think how many pleasures you have now that you didn't have when you were a baby! And as you continue to grow up and change, you will find that there are even more new pleasures!

It's hard sometimes to change, but it is how God made us and~just like everything God made~it is good.

It is hard to explain to you how good some of these new pleasures will be, just like it is hard to explain to a baby how good pizza is. These new

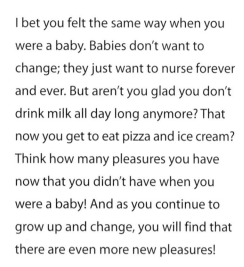

And, let me tell you, there is something a lot better than pizza coming your way!

pleasures will be so good that you will be tempted to have more of them than you should. Or tempted to have them at times when you shouldn't. Just like now sometimes you may be tempted to eat too much ice cream. Or to eat ice cream when you should be eating your lunch. You didn't have that temptation when you were a baby, because you didn't know anything about ice cream. With new pleasures, come new temptations.

But with new temptations also comes new grace! God can help you enjoy the new pleasures in a way that pleases and honors Him.

And, let me tell you, there is something a lot better than pizza coming your way!

TRUE *Beauty*

Write out a Bible verse here that shows you what true beauty is.

"No temptation has overtaken you that is not common to man. God is faithful, and He will not let you be tempted beyond your ability, but with the temptation He will also provide the way of escape, that you may be able to endure it."

—1 Corinthians 10:13, ESV

One new temptation you will have as you grow up is to dress or act in ways that do not honor your private parts. There will be a while before you have a husband to admire your special beauty and it will be tempting to have some other guy admire you. You probably won't be tempted to go around naked, but you will learn that there are ways to draw attention and admiration to your body without being naked.

Temptations are a kind of trial or test.

Instead of being like a spelling test that shows what is in your mind, these tests show what is in your heart. But remember, God is faithful. He won't let you be tested "above your grade level." The trial may be hard, it may feel too hard, but pray and ask God for help. He can give you the strength you need to pass the test.

God gives these new pleasures because He is good. Satan tries to use these new pleasures to get you to sin because he is evil. Who will you listen to when temptation comes?

Mysterious ME

From what you have read in the case of the baby who never grew up why not use this page to write or draw something about yourself

Chapter 10:

THE CASE OF THE GUMSHOE WHO WAS ALWAYS DYING

You might be asking, what in the world is a gumshoe? And that's a good question. Though if you were Amelia Bedelia you wouldn't ask, you would just come up with your own idea and it would be hilarious. You might, for instance, think that a gumshoe was a shoe made out of bubble gum. Or that it was a type of gum made out of shoes. And, like Amelia Bedelia, you would be wrong... though hilarious!

It's actually a long story, but I bet you like stories, so do let me tell you. Deep in the tropics, in many parts of the world, there is a special sort of tree. If you cut a small strip into this tree, it will "bleed" a white liquid. For hundreds and maybe thousands of years, the natives of these lands have been collecting the liquid in buckets and drying it until it becomes thick and

stretchy, much like chewed gum. Then they could do many things with it, like make balls. They would also stick their feet into it while it was still a liquid and let it dry on their feet. They would do this several times, adding layer on top of layer, until it got thick enough. Then they would peel the stuff off their feet, smoke it to harden it and wear it like a shoe.

Columbus brought some of this stuff back with him on one of his trips and over the years, people experimented with it. It was often called rubber or gum rubber. People especially liked the idea of making shoes with it. Back then shoes had hard soles (the sole is the part

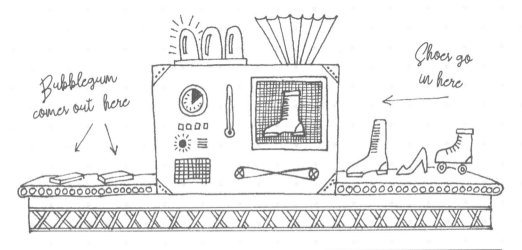

Bubblegum comes out here

Shoes go in here

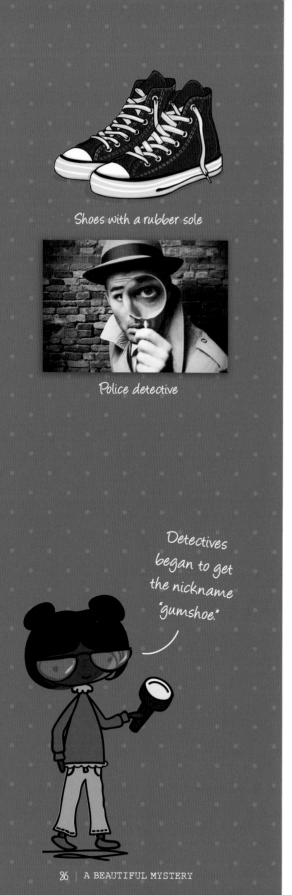

Shoes with a rubber sole

Police detective

Detectives began to get the nickname "gumshoe."

of the shoe that touches the ground) and they were often uncomfortable or expensive. People began making shoes which had soles made out of this gum rubber. And can you possibly guess what these shoes were called, oh, detective friend of mine?

That's right, gumshoes! Kind of like our tennis shoes or sneakers, they had a soft bottom to the shoe.

But that's only half the story…. Like I said, I hope you like long stories.

Well, the thing people noticed about these shoes was how quiet they were. With hard-soled shoes you could hear people coming by their footsteps, but now they could sneak up on you and surprise you. Bad guys like robbers might wear gumshoes so they could break into someone's home and go quietly around the house stealing things without anyone hearing them. But bad guys aren't the only ones that have to be sneaky. People that want to catch the bad guys have to be sneaky too. So police officers and detectives became associated with gumshoes and they, especially detectives, began to get the nickname "gumshoe." And it stuck even when people stopped wearing gumshoes. Maybe you have a nickname like this. A name that started when you were a child and just stayed even when you grew up.

So that was a long story to tell you that a gumshoe is a detective. And since you have been a detective with me this whole book, you are a gumshoe! Now who would have guessed? Not Amelia Bedelia, that's for sure.

Before I tell you about the gumshoe who was always dying, let's talk a little about clothes. Clothes are good for many reasons. They keep us warm, they protect us from too much sun, they are pretty and fun to dress up in. But their most important job is that they honor our bodies. They show that the best parts of our body are kept for someone special. Much like that reserved sign on the special table at the wedding.

Modest clothes honor the beauty of our private parts in several ways:

They cover the parts of our body that should be covered and they cover them completely. Not like lace that half covers them and half shows them. And not like see-through material that lets them be seen in a blurry way.

They cover them all the time, when we sit down, when we bend over, *when we take a walk in the breeze. There are some clothes that are only modest if you stand just so. These clothes may be modest for a statue, but since you are not a statue, they will not honor your body well!*

They are not so tight that they show the exact shape of the parts of the body that should be covered. Because not just your skin, but the shape of your private parts is beautiful and special and reserved.

It may not be easy to find such clothes. When you find them, they might not be the clothes you like the best. They're probably not going to be what everyone else is wearing. You may feel weird for dressing differently. Other girls may get a lot more attention from boys and you may feel left out. But honoring your body is important. It is not just something you do when it is easy or when you like it. It may mean, gumshoe, that you have to die to self, to what you want and what you like. But dying to self is a large part of the Christian life. It is something we have to do every day. It is the only way you can live for Christ.

"If anyone desires to come after Me, let him deny himself, and take up his cross, and follow Me."
—Matthew 16:24b

A cross is not a fun thing to take up. A cross is something you die on. It is like saying, "Take up your guillotine or electric chair and follow me." Some people think that if you are a Christian, God promises you a wonderful life. But instead He tells you to die, to suffer, to do what is hard. But look at what He does promise:

> " For whoever desires to save his life will lose it, but whoever loses his life for My sake will find it."
> —Matthew 16:25 (NKVJ)

How can you find something by losing it? Because you lose it by giving it to God who gives you back something so much better than what you lost. There are many little and big ways we die to self. Dressing to please God, not ourselves, is one small way that we die to self. This doesn't mean you can't wear clothes you like, it just means that can't be what is most important to you. Sometimes you will find cute, modest clothes that you are excited about wearing. That's wonderful! But sometimes you won't. And then you will have to choose between what you like and what is modest. That's hard. Sometimes that is very hard. Especially if other people around you are making different choices and getting attention you would like to have. But it can be choices like this which show who you are really living for.

Because you are young, your parents probably make this choice for you. They tell you what you can wear and what

What will you do with your freedom when it comes?

you can't. But you still have a choice. Are you going to sweetly submit to their rules?

Or are you going to resist or try to punish them by pouting and having a bad attitude?

Let me tell you something that may sound really bizarre…or maybe like something that happened yesterday. There are girls who are excited about being missionaries or mothers one day, both of which are hard jobs where you have to do what is best for others and not what you want. There are even girls who say that they would be martyrs and die if they had to. But these same girls sometimes complain or throw a fit when their parents say they can't wear those jeans or that dress. How do I know? Because I used to be that girl. It's easy to talk about dying for Christ, it is hard to actually do it.

As you grow up, you will have more and more freedom to choose your own clothes. That's a change most children are excited about! However, with that freedom, comes responsibility. Freedom for a Christian does not mean doing whatever you want. With freedom comes the responsibility to make decisions that please God. What will you do with your freedom when it comes?

TRUE Beauty

Write out a Bible verse here that shows you what true beauty is.

A CLUE
To chew on

"...every branch that bears fruit He prunes, that it may bear more fruit."

—John 15:2b

Prune is another word for cut. In pruning, parts of the tree are cut off so that the rest of the tree can bear more good things. It is a lot like what happens to the tree from the tropics we were talking about. People cut it, which hurts the tree, but then it gives this special liquid that can be turned into rubber. By being hurt, it can help people, it can give them balls to play with and shoes to wear and even tires for their cars!

Nature all around us teaches us this lesson of bringing good out of pain and loss.

Flowers have to be crushed before they can give us perfume. Carbon has to be under pressure and heated to 800 degrees before it gives us a diamond. Jesus is the perfect example of this. He had to die so that we can live.

This is how we can rejoice even when life is hard, because we know that God uses trials to bring good. We will see bits of that good here on earth, but we have to wait until the wedding party starts to really know how much life has come out of death. Until then, gumshoe, live by faith. Live in hope. And keep dying every day.

From what you have read in the case of the gumshoe who was always dying, why not use this page to write or draw something about yourself

Chapter 11:

MYSTERIES OF THE SECRET GARDEN

You may have read a book called *The Secret Garden*. It is a fictional story about an orphaned girl named Mary who goes to live with her uncle in a big house called Misselthwaite Manor. The house is surrounded by gardens: vegetable gardens, flower gardens, herb gardens. One day a maid tells Mary about a secret garden, far lovelier than all the others. However, it has been so long since anyone went inside and the place has become so overgrown that no one remembers exactly where the garden is. Worse, this garden had a tall wall all around it and the only way in was through a door, but the door was locked tight and the key thrown away.

Like any child, like any detective, Mary was very curious about this secret garden. She explored and explored, hoping to find it. One day a robin came along and acted like it wanted to be her friend. As she watched, it hopped on a mound of dirt that a dog had been digging up. It seemed like it was pecking around for a worm but then Mary saw something metal sticking out of the dirt and she bent down and found a key. An old, rusty key. She didn't know what it went to, but she kept it.

Another day the robin helped her find the garden. It perched on top of a wall overgrown with ivy singing the sweetest song. As Mary walked around the wall, a breeze came along and the ivy started swinging back and forth like a curtain in front of a fan. That's when Mary caught sight of the door knob. She reached through the layers of ivy and grasped it with her hand. She took her key and used all her strength to turn it in the old, rusty lock. It turned and the door to the secret garden slowly creaked opened.

Inside was the sweetest, most mysterious-looking place anyone could imagine. There were rose bushes that were like little trees. There were rose vines that had climbed over other trees,

going from tree to tree like bridges, and hanging down on the sides like curtains. The paths were mostly overgrown but Mary could still see stone seats and moss-covered flower pots peeking out of the underbrush. It was winter now so the roses were dead, adding to the sense of mystery. Mary, the book says, felt as if she had found a world all her own.

A secret garden makes a perfect mystery! It is exciting to find something other people don't know about. The Bible tells us about a secret garden. It's not the Garden of Eden and it's not the Garden of Gethsemane. This garden actually is lots of gardens with lots of names. In fact, one of them has your name! But before I tell you about that secret garden, let me tell you about one more thing that God did to make men and women happy together.

Remember the nursery rhyme about Jack Sprat? How many men and women were sharing the plate of food? There was ONE man and ONE woman, wasn't there? There was Jack and Joan. There wasn't Jack and Jim and Joan. What do you think would have happened if there had been two men eating the lean meat and only one woman eating the fat? Why, there would have been fighting and envy and resentment! There wouldn't be as much to go around and they would argue over it.

One man learned this the hard way. You may have read of Jacob in the Bible. Jacob had not just one wife, but two. He married one woman named Leah

God knew that people start fighting easily so he made marriage to be between one man and one woman

and then he married her sister Rachel. There was jealousy and arguing big time in that family.

God knew that people start fighting easily so He made marriage to be between *one* man and *one* woman. This doesn't mean that husbands and wives never argue, but it makes things easier.

God desires for people to be happy.

However, Satan hates to see people happy so he tries to mess things up. One way Satan does this is to tempt men to look at other women besides their wives and think about how pretty they are and wish they could see more of their beauty. Jesus teaches us in Matthew 5 that this is very wrong:

"You have heard that it was said by them of old time, You shall not commit adultery: But I say unto you, That whosoever looks on a woman to lust after her has committed adultery with her already in his heart," Matthew 5: 27-28, KJV 2000.

Adultery is treating other people like they are your husband or wife when they are not. The Bible says it is very wrong. To lust is to want something you should not have. This person may

TRUE
Beauty

Write out a Bible verse here that shows you what true beauty is.

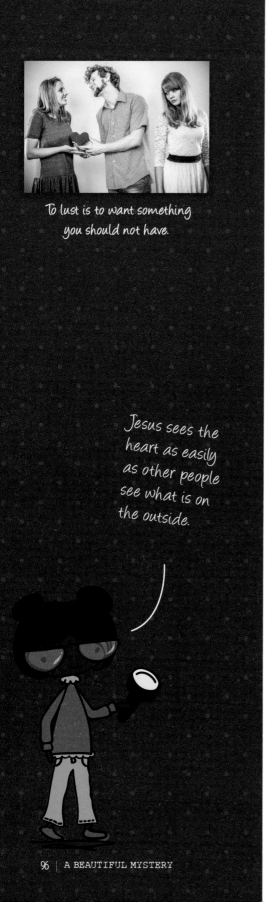

To lust is to want something you should not have.

Jesus sees the heart as easily as other people see what is on the outside.

not do anything bad that people can see, but in their heart they are thinking all sorts of bad thoughts. But Jesus sees the heart as easily as other people see what is on the outside. Jesus is saying that a man should be content in his heart with his wife's beauty and not want to enjoy the hidden beauty of other women.

Satan also tempts women. He tempts them to want other men to enjoy their beauty. Instead of being satisfied with the husbands God gave them, they want more. They feel that it's not enough for one man to notice them and admire them, they want lots of men to notice and admire them. It might seem to make sense that if it is nice to have one man admire your beauty, then it would be even nicer to have lots of men admiring you. But God's Word says it is not nicer. And the world around us shows us that it is not. There are models and actresses who have millions of men think about how beautiful they are. But these women are often hurting and lonely. Models and beautiful actresses are often treated very badly by men. They smile big for cameras because they are paid to, but often inside they feel empty. The people who admire their beauty don't love them and that is one of the saddest things.

When men and women give into these temptations, marriages become unhappy. Men become discontent with their wives. Women become jealous of each other. Instead of happily sharing the same plate of food, husbands and wives start trying to eat off other people's plates of food and that starts fights.

The greatest happiness comes from being admired by a husband who loves you and is committed to you for the rest of his life. It's not the number of people who admire a girl's beauty that makes her happy, it is how much she is loved by the person who admires her.

God gave a book of the Bible that is mostly about a man admiring a woman's beauty. It is Song of Solomon and it talks a lot about how beautiful King Solomon thought his bride was. He describes her whole body and compares it to the most beautiful things he could think of. We don't have a picture of this woman, maybe you wouldn't think she was so very pretty, but he did because he loved her. In Song of Solomon 4:12 he wrote:

> *"A garden locked is my sister, my bride …"* ESV

He called her a garden. Gardens are beautiful and he thought she was beautiful. But he also called her a locked garden. That meant that she wasn't for everyone, she had a wall around her with a locked door. Not just anyone could come into her garden. Solomon was singing because she had let him in and let him enjoy her beauty. Now this doesn't mean there was a wall of stone around her! Or that she had roses growing out of her ears! Gardens and walls are just ways of thinking about it. It's an analogy.

Well, can you guess now what the garden is with your name on it? It's your body! Your body is a lovely garden, far lovelier even than the secret rose garden! Modesty is kind of like a wall around your body, keeping other people out of the most special places. Some parts of your beauty are for everyone to see, but other parts are covered by clothes and will be for a husband who loves you to enjoy one day. And what a special day that will be! It is the stuff of songs!

MAN TO WOMAN:

"Behold, you are beautiful, my love, behold, you are beautiful! ...

You have captivated my heart, my sister, my bride ...

A garden locked is my sister, my bride, a spring locked, a fountain sealed.

Your shoots are an orchard of pomegranates with all choicest fruits ...

A garden fountain, a well of living water ..."

WOMAN TO MAN:

"Let my beloved come to his garden, and eat its choicest fruits."

—Excerpts from Song of Solomon 4, ESV

Many boys will tell you that they love you to try to get you to let them into the private places of your garden, they may do many nice things and say many nicer things and make you feel wonderful. But wait. Be patient. Say no. Keep your garden locked until you are married to a man you know loves you. Then give him the key to your garden, let him and him only into the special places of your body. It may be hard to wait that long. But trust God. Believe that He is good and wants good things for you. There will be boys who won't want to wait. But remember how beautiful and special your body is and that it is worth waiting for. Even when other girls are showing off their bodies and getting a lot of attention and you feel left out, trust and obey God. His ways are often mysterious, but His ways are best.

From what you have read in mysteries of the secret garden, why not use this page to write or draw something about yourself

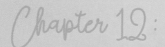 Chapter 12:

THE SAD CASE OF THE REJECTED PARTY CLOTHES

Do you remember the story of Cinderella? Cinderella wanted to go to the ball but she didn't have a dress to wear. Then a fairy godmother made her a very special, magical dress and she was so happy. She looked beautiful and the prince fell in love with her and they lived happily ever after.

But what would have happened if she had refused to wear the dress and had gone to the ball in her torn and dirty dress? They wouldn't have even let her into the palace and she would have never met the prince. Cinderella's story would have ended, "And she lived sadly ever after."

Jesus told a story in Matthew 22 about a man who rejected clothes more wonderful even than Cinderella's fairy tale ballgown and the Bible says this man lived sadly ever after. Why would anyone do something like that? This is our last mystery to solve. Let's first review the facts of the case:

There was a king whose son was getting married and to celebrate, he gave a big, fancy party and invited people to come. But at first no one

wanted to come! Some people said they were too busy. Others were mean to the king's servants who were handing out the invitations. When the king heard this, he was FURIOUS. So furious that he sent out his army and destroyed all those people. Then he told his servants to go to the poor places in the city, find the people who lived in the streets and in the dumps, the people most kings wouldn't want at their party, and invite them to come.

The King knew that these people were poor and would not have the right clothes to wear but he still wanted them to come so he made clothes for them—beautiful, amazing clothes. And they wouldn't disappear at midnight like Cinderella's dress; no, these clothes were very special, they would last forever. But when the king came to the party, he saw a man who was still dressed in his old, smelly work clothes. He could have had the beautiful clothes the King had bought for his guests, but he was rebellious and wanted to do things his way. The King asked the man, "Why aren't you wearing the special clothes I gave?" Before he saw the king he probably thought he was just fine the way he was. But when he saw the King who was wearing the most amazing,

beautiful, dazzling clothes he had ever imagined and looked down at his own shabby clothes, he couldn't think of a single thing to say. He had been very foolish not to take the clothes the King had offered him. Now it was too late and the King ordered the rebellious man to be tied up and thrown out of the palace.

This story is called a parable. Jesus told it to teach us something. Let's look in the Bible for clues about what it means.

Clue #1:

Jesus starts this story by saying "The kingdom of heaven is like a certain king…" So we know that this story is really about the kingdom of heaven. And who is king in heaven? God is! So God is similar to the King in this story.

The King knew that these people were poor and would not have the right clothes to wear … so he made clothes for them.

Clue #2:

When Jesus ends this story, he says the man will be thrown out "into outer darkness, where there will be weeping and gnashing of teeth." This is how the Bible describes hell. So if outside the party is hell, then what do you think the party is supposed to be like? That's right, heaven!

Jesus calls the party clothes the "wedding garment." I bet when you go to a wedding, you get dressed up and wear special clothes. Now, what is something like a wedding garment that people would need to wear in order to get into heaven? Here are some clues from other places in the Bible:

Clue #3:

Isaiah 61:10: says, "[God] has clothed me with the garments of salvation,

He has covered me with the robe of righteousness…"

TRUE Beauty

Write out a Bible verse here that shows you what true beauty is.

Old, smelly work clothes

Our best clothes are not good enough

Cinderella's ball gown

Christ's righteousness is a gift, kind of like Cinderella's ball gown was a gift

Clue #4:

Revelation 7 talks about people in heaven wearing white robes. Jesus' disciple, John, asked about the people in the white robes and was told that they had made them white in the blood of Jesus.

To get into heaven we need Christ's righteousness. That's the wedding garment. It is because Jesus died and because of the blood He shed that He can wash us clean from sin and guilt. When we are cleansed by Jesus from sin we are cleaner and whiter than any snow you've ever seen. It is as if there is a beautiful robe put on our hearts. But what are the old, smelly work clothes the man was wearing like?

Clue #5:

"all our righteousnesses are as filthy rags." (Isaiah 64:6)

The man in the parable was wearing his own righteousness instead of the righteousness that God gives. But God says our righteousness is like filthy rags. No one wants that at their party! And God can't have that in heaven. You can not get into heaven by your own goodness. But that's exactly what most people try to do. They know they aren't perfect, but they think that if they try a little harder, they can be

Your goodness is nothing but old stinky clothes. It can never enter heaven.

good enough. But the Bible says that is impossible.

Clue #6:

"There is none righteous, no, not one…" Romans 3:10

If no one is righteous, then we can deduce that you and I are not righteous. Maybe you would like to know how to have your heart dressed in the robe of Christ's righteousness so that you will be welcome in heaven. It's very easy. You just have to do what the man in Jesus' story should've done. He should have realized that his own clothes weren't good enough for such a nice party. Maybe his clothes were better than other people's clothes but this was a really nice party.

You also need to realize that no matter how good you are or even how much better you are than other people, you are not good enough to go to heaven. Your goodness is nothing but old stinky clothes. It can never enter heaven.

Then you need to believe God's promise to give Christ's righteousness to anyone who asks. Christ's righteousness is a gift, kind of like Cinderella's ball gown was a gift. Ask God for His righteousness. The Bible says that he will not turn anyone away, he will never say no. Because He has decided to throw a very big party!

A CLUE To chew on

"All our righteousnesses are as filthy rags."

—Isaiah 64:6

Trying to go to heaven dressed in your own goodness would be like Cinderella telling the fairy godmother, "No, thank you. I like my old dress better. I'll just smooth the skirt out a little and try to lick this ink stain off my sleeve and I'll be ready to go to the ball without your help."

Cinderella knew better than that, she knew enough to be grateful for the beautiful blue ball gown. But most people are more like the man in Jesus' story. He was too proud to wear someone else's clothes and most people are too proud to ask God for Christ's righteousness. Instead they try to be kind enough, try to read their Bibles enough, try to obey their parents enough, try to be modest enough and think that will make them good enough. But you might as well try to lick away an ink stain as to make your heart good by doing any of that. Only Christ was truly good and only Christ's goodness can make your heart good.

Mysterious
ME

From what you have read in the case of the rejected party clothes, why not use this page to write or draw something about yourself

The Beauty and Mystery of God

"One thing I have desired of the LORD,
That will I seek: That I may dwell in the house
of the LORD All the days of my life,
To behold the beauty of the LORD,
And to inquire in His temple." Psalm 27:4

"The Mighty One, God the LORD,
Has spoken and called the earth
From the rising of the sun to its going down.
Out of Zion, the perfection of beauty,
God will shine forth." Psalm 50:1-2

He is the radiance of the glory of God
and the exact imprint of his nature,
and he upholds the universe by the word of his
power. Hebrews 1:3, ESV

Honor and majesty are before Him; Strength and
beauty are in His sanctuary. Psalm 96:6

"Oh, the depth of the riches both of the wisdom and
knowledge of God! How unsearchable are
His judgments and His ways past finding out!"
Romans 11:33

"Can you search out the deep things of God?
Can you find out the limits of the Almighty?
They are higher than heaven-what can you do?
Deeper than Sheol-what can you know?
Their measure is longer than the earth
And broader than the sea." Job 11:7-9

"For My thoughts are not your thoughts,
Nor are your ways My ways," says the LORD.
"For as the heavens are higher than the earth,
So are My ways higher than your ways,
And My thoughts than your thoughts." Isaiah 55:8-9

"And without controversy great is the mystery of
godliness: God was manifested in the flesh,
Justified in the Spirit, Seen by angels,
Preached among the Gentiles, Believed on in the
world, Received up in glory." 1 Timothy 3:16

"But we speak the wisdom of God in a mystery, the
hidden wisdom which God ordained before the ages
for our glory…" 1 Corinthians 2:7

"but in the days of the sounding of the seventh
angel, when he is about to sound, the mystery of God
would be finished, as He declared to His servants
the prophets." Revelation 10:7

Heather Thieneman

Heather Thieneman lives in Kentucky in the United States of America. She works at a private school and belongs to the Reformed Baptist Church of Louisville. Previously she has written, *What's Up With the Fig Leaves?*, a book on the principles and purposes of modesty for adults.

Endorsements

In *A Beautiful Mystery*, Heather addresses the topics of our bodies, modesty, and true beauty through the lens of Scripture. This book would be best read by a mother and daughter and used as a springboard for conversation. I found it helpful myself and was pointed to Christ repeatedly.

Sharon Mañón, Homeschooling mom, Louisville, Kentucky

Modesty, inner beauty and being clothed in Christ's righteousness are important topics for young girls. Heather Thieneman's book, *A Beautiful Mystery*, is full of biblical reminders for pre-teens to take note of. It will be a helpful book.

Carolyn Poon, Homeschooling mother, Singapore

PAGE Nº.	PHOTO DESCRIPTION	CREDIT/LICENSE
12	Pregnant lady	Heather Mount on Unsplash
14	The Hanging Gardens in Babylon	Ferdinand Knab (1834-1902) [Public domain]
14	Lighthouse of Alexandria	Mohammed Mahdy [CC BY-SA 4.0]
20	Lady's Eyes	Eric Ward on Unsplash
22	Tux the cat	Author's photo
22	Tuxedo	Viespire Travel on Unsplash
22	Skunk	Bryan Padron on Unsplash
22	Queen Anne's Lace	Jo Naylor Flickr [CC BY 2.0]
23	Tent	Josh Hild on Unsplash
26	Lady in the Mirror	Taylor Smith on Unsplash
29	Daisies	Micheile Henderson // Visual Stories on Unsplash
29	Grape Hyacinth	Annie Spratt on Unsplash
29	Hydrangea	Annie Spratt on Unsplash
29	Iris	Alpsdake [CC BY-SA 3.0]
31	Snow White	Photo Screen capture, Flickr (CC BY 2.0)
32	Sunrise Landscape	Artem Sapegin on Unsplash
33	Stop Girl	Isaiah Rustad on Unsplash
38	Wedding photo	Todd Ruth on Unsplash
44	Adam & Eve Clothing	Sincerely Media on Unsplash
45	Muddy Boots	Annie Spratt on Unsplash
45	Sherlock Holmes	Employee(s) of Universal Studios [Public domain]
46	Clothes	Artem Beliaikin on Unsplash
48	Adam & Eve Stained Glass Window	David Dixon, Geograph, [CC BY-SA 2.0]
49	Apple Tree	Marina Khrapova on Unsplash
58	Heather in a her favourite nightgown	Author's photo
63	Amelia bedelia book	Author: Peggy Parish, published by HarperCollins
64	John Knox	William Holl [Public domain]
64	Queen Elizabeth	Formerly attributed to George Gower [Public domain]
64	King James I	John de Critz [Public domain]
66	Flowers on a Table	Annie Spratt on Unsplash
67	Girl in Jumper	Annie Spratt on Unsplash
71	Jack Sprat and his wife	Frederick Richardson [Public domain]
73	Bedroom	Chuttersnap on Unsplash
78	Sleeping Woman	Wes Hicks on Unsplash
79	Peaches	Ian Baldwin on Unsplash
80	Ice-Cream Sundae	Emile Mbunzama on Unsplash
80-81	Pizza	Brenna Huff on Unsplash
92	Walled Garden	Annie Spratt on Unsplash
93	Robin	Chris Child on Unsplash
104	Cinderella	mydisneyadventures [CC BY 2.0]
	Cartoon Girls	Based on image by: ID 21864605 © Virinaflora	Dreamstime.com

Photo information

LICENSE DEFINITIONS:
CC BY 2.0 – https://creativecommons.org/licenses/by/2.0)
CC BY 3.0 – https://creativecommons.org/licenses/by/3.0)
CC BY-SA 4.0 – https://creativecommons.org/licenses/by-sa/4.0)